UNDER THE TREE

"And over and over I tried to see
Some of us walking under the tree

.   .   .

And how it looks when I am there."
FROM *On the Hill*

UNDER THE TREE

ELIZABETH MADOX ROBERTS

With an Afterword by William H. Slavick

THE UNIVERSITY PRESS OF KENTUCKY

Enlarged edition, illustrated by F.D. Bedford

Reprinted by arrangement with Viking Penguin, Inc., by

THE UNIVERSITY PRESS OF KENTUCKY

Scholarly publisher for the Commonwealth,
serving Bellarmine College, Berea College, Centre
College of Kentucky, Eastern Kentucky University,
The Filson Club, Georgetown College, Kentucky
Historical Society, Kentucky State University,
Morehead State University, Murray State University,
Northern Kentucky University, Transylvania University,
University of Kentucky, University of Louisville,
and Western Kentucky University.

Editorial and Sales Offices: Lexington, Kentucky 40506-0024

Library of Congress Cataloging-in-Publication Data

Roberts, Elizabeth Madox, 1881-1941.
  Under the tree.

  Summary: An illustrated collection of poems
reflecting the activities and impressions of childhood.
    1. Children's poetry, American. [1. American poetry]
I. Slavick, William H. II. Bedford, F.D., ill. III. Title
PS3535.0172U6 1985   811'.52   85-8647
ISBN 0-8131-1561-2

To my father
SIMPSON ROBERTS

CONTENTS

THE SKY

I saw a shadow on the ground
And heard a bluejay going by;
A shadow went across the ground,
And I looked up and saw the sky.

It hung up on the poplar tree,
But while I looked it did not stay;
It gave a tiny sort of jerk
And moved a little bit away.

And farther on and farther on
It moved and never seemed to stop,
I think it must be tied with chains
And something pulls it from the top.

It never has come down again,
And every time I look to see,
The sky is always slipping back
And getting far away from me.

THE CORNFIELD

I went across the pasture lot
When not a one was watching me.
Away beyond the cattle barns
I climbed a little crooked tree.

And I could look down on the field
And see the corn and how it grows
Across the world and up and down
In very straight and even rows.

And far away and far away—
I wonder if the farmer man
Knows all about the corn and how
It comes together like a fan.

MILKING TIME

When supper time is almost come,
But not quite here, I cannot wait,
And so I take my china mug
And go down by the milking gate.

The cow is always eating shucks
And spilling off the little silk.
Her purple eyes are big and soft—
She always smells like milk.

And Father takes my mug from me,
And then he makes the stream come out.
I see it going in my mug
And foaming all about.

And when it's piling very high,
And when some little streams commence
To run and drip along the sides,
He hands it to me through the fence.

IN MY PILLOW

When Mother or Father turns down the light,
I like to look into my pillow at night.

Some people call them dreams, but for me
They are things I look down in my pillow and see.

I saw some birds, as many as four,
They were all blue wings and nothing else more.

Without any head and without any feet,
Just blue wings flying over a street.

And almost every night I see
A little brown bowl that can talk to me,

A nice little bowl that laughs and sings,
And ever so many other things.

Sometimes they are plainer than I can say,
And while I am waking they go away.

And when nobody is coming by,
I feel my pillow all over and try

And try to feel the pretty things,
The little brown bowl and the flying wings.

MISS KATE-MARIE

And it was Sunday everywhere,
And Father pinned a rose on me
And said he guessed he'd better take
Me down to see Miss Kate-Marie.

And when I went it all turned out
To be a Sunday school, and there
Miss Kate-Marie was very good
And let me stand beside her chair.

Her hat was made of yellow lace;
Her dress was very soft and thin,
And when she talked her little tongue
Was always wriggling out and in.

I liked to smell my pretty rose;
I liked to feel her silky dress.
She held a very little book
And asked the things for us to guess.

She asked me about Who-made-y-God,
And never seemed to fuss or frown;
I liked to watch her little tongue
And see it wriggle up and down.

THE TWINS

The two-ones is the name for it,
And that is what it ought to be,
But when you say it very fast
It makes your lips say *twins,* you see.

When I was just a little thing,
About the year before the last,
I called it two-ones all the time,
But now I always say it fast.

THE WOODPECKER

The woodpecker pecked out a little round hole
And made him a house in the telephone pole.

One day when I watched he poked out his head,
And he had on a hood and a collar of red.

When the streams of rain pour out of the sky,
And the sparkles of lightning go flashing by,

And the big, big wheels of thunder roll,
He can snuggle back in the telephone pole.

THE STAR

A Song

O little one away so far,
You cannot hear me when I sing.

You cannot tell me what you are,
I cannot tell you anything.

THE BUTTERBEAN TENT

All through the garden I went and went,
And I walked in under the butterbean tent.

The poles leaned up like a good tepee
And made a nice little house for me.

I had a hard brown clod for a seat,
And all outside was a cool green street.

A little green worm and a butterfly
And a cricket-like thing that could hop went by.

Hidden away there were flocks and flocks
Of bugs that could go like little clocks.

Such a good day it was when I spent
A long, long while in the butterbean tent.

BIG BROTHER

Our brother Clarence goes to school.
He has a slate and a blue school-bag.
He has a book and a copybook
And a scholar's companion and a little slate rag.

He knows a boy named Joe B. Kirk,
And he learns about c-a-t cat,
And how to play one-two-sky-blue,
And how to make a football out of a hat.

We climb up on the fence and gate
And watch until he's small and dim,
Far up the street, and he looks back
To see if we keep on watching him.

MR. WELLS

On Sunday morning, then he comes
To church, and everybody smells
The blacking and the toilet soap
And camphor balls from Mr. Wells.

He wears his whiskers in a bunch,
And wears his glasses on his head.
I mustn't call him Old Man Wells—
No matter—that's what Father said.

And when the little blacking smells
And camphor balls and soap begin,
I do not have to look to know
That Mr. Wells is coming in.

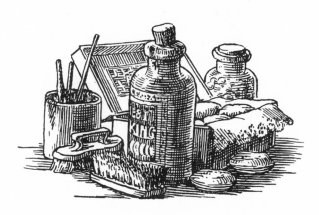

DICK AND WILL

Our brother says that Will was born
The very day that Dickie came;
When one is four the other is,
And all their birthdays are the same.

Their coats and waists are just alike;
They have their hats together, too.
They sleep together in one bed,
And Will can put on Dickie's shoe.

But they are not the same at all;
Two different boys they have to be,
For Dick can play in Mother's room
When Will is climbing in a tree.

Or maybe Will is on the porch
To cry because he stubbed his toe,
And Dick is laughing by the gate
And watching ants go in a row.

FIREFLY

A Song

A little light is going by,
Is going up to see the sky,
A little light with wings.

I never could have thought of it,
To have a little bug all lit
And made to go on wings.

LITTLE RAIN

When I was making myself a game
Up in the garden, a little rain came.

It fell down quick in a sort of rush,
And I crawled back under the snowball bush.

I could hear the big drops hit the ground
And see little puddles of dust fly round.

A chicken came till the rain was gone;
He had just a very few feathers on.

He shivered a little under his skin,
And then he shut his eyeballs in.

Even after the rain had begun to hush
It kept on raining up in the bush.

One big flat drop came sliding down,
And a ladybug that was red and brown

Was up on a little stem waiting there,
And I got some rain in my hair.

THE PULPIT

On Sunday when I go to church
I wear my dress that's trimmed with lace.
I sit beside my mother and
Am very quiet in my place.

When Dr. Brown is reading hymns
To make the people want to sing,
Or when he preaches loud and makes
The shivery bells begin to ring,

I watch the little pulpit house—
It isn't very tall or wide—
And then I wonder all about
The little ones that live inside.

When Dr. Brown has preached enough,
And when he is about to stop,
He stands behind the little house
And shuts the Bible on the top.

I wonder if *they* sit inside,
And if *they* cook and walk up stairs.
I wonder if *they* have a cat
And say some kind of little prayers.

I wonder if *they're* ever scared
Because the bedroom lamp goes out,
And what their little dreams are like
And what *they* wonder all about.

ON THE HILL

Mother said that we could go
Up on the hill where the strawberries grow.

And while I was there I looked all down,
Over the trees and over the town.

I saw the field where the big boys play,
And the roads that come from every way,

The courthouse place where the wagons stop,
And the bridge and the scales and the blacksmith shop.

The church steeple looked very tall and thin,
And I found the house that we live in.

I saw it under the poplar tree,
And I bent my head and tried to see

Our house when the rain is over it,
And how it looks when the lamps are lit.

I saw the swing from up on the hill,
The ropes were hanging very still.

And over and over I tried to see
Some of us walking under the tree,

And the children playing everywhere,
And how it looks when I am there.

But Dickie said, "Come on, let's race";
And Will had found the strawberry place.

AUTUMN

Dick and Will and Charles and I
Were playing it was election day,
And I was running for president,
And Dick was a band that was going to play,

And Charles and Will were a street parade,
But Clarence came and said that he
Was going to run for president,
And I could run for school-trustee.

He made some flags for Charles and Will
And a badge to go on Dickie's coat.
He stood some cornstalks by the fence
And had them for the men that vote.

Then he climbed on a box and made a speech
To the cornstalk men that were in a row.
It was all about the dem-o-crats,
And "I de-fy any man to show."

And "I de-fy any man to say."
And all about "It's a big disgrace."
He spoke his speech out very loud
And shook his fist in a cornstalk's face.

THE PILASTER

The church has pieces jutting out
Where corners of the walls begin.
I have one for my little house,
And I can feel myself go in.

I feel myself go in the bricks,
And I can see myself in there.
I'm always waiting all alone,
I'm sitting on a little chair.

And I am sitting very still,
And I am waiting on and on
For something that is never there,
For something that is gone.

THE RABBIT

When they said the time to hide was mine,
I hid back under a thick grape vine.

And while I was still for the time to pass,
A little gray thing came out of the grass.

He hopped his way through the melon bed
And sat down close by a cabbage head.

He sat down close where I could see,
And his big still eyes looked hard at me,

His big eyes bursting out of the rim,
And I looked back very hard at him.

CRESCENT MOON

And Dick said, "Look what I have found!"
And when we saw we danced around,
And made our feet just tip the ground.

We skipped our toes and sang, "Oh-lo.
Oh-who, oh-who, oh what do you know!
Oh-who, oh-hi, oh-loo, kee-lo!"

We clapped our hands and sang, "Oh-ee!"
It made us jump and laugh to see
The little new moon above the tree.

THE RICHEST WOMAN IN THE WORLD

She has some tongs made out of pearl
To poke the fire and make it burn.
She pours the milk in diamond crocks
And churns the cream in a silver churn.

And when she's tired she has a stool;
It's made of jade with pearls set in it.
She sits down here and wipes her face
And gets her breath a minute.

On Saturday she stirs the cake
With gold, and when the water is hot,
She kills the hen with a golden axe
And scalds her in a golden pot.

She chops the meat with a golden knife
And cooks it in a golden skillet.
For coal she has a golden hod.
There is always a plenty to fill it.

FATHER'S STORY

We put more coal on the big red fire,
And while we are waiting for dinner to cook,
Our father comes and tells us about
A story that he has read in a book.

And Charles and Will and Dick and I
And all of us but Clarence are there.
And some of us sit on Father's legs,
But one has to sit on the little red chair.

And when we are sitting very still,
He sings us a song or tells a piece;
He sings Dan Tucker Went to Town,
Or he tells us about the golden fleece.

He tells about the golden wool,
And some of it is about a boy
Named Jason, and about a ship,
And some is about a town called Troy.

And while he is telling or singing it through,
I stand by his arm, for that is my place.
And I push my fingers into his skin
To make little dents in his big rough face.

CHRISTMAS MORNING

If Bethlehem were here today,
Or this were very long ago,
There wouldn't be a winter time
Nor any cold or snow.

I'd run out through the garden gate,
And down along the pasture walk;
And off beside the cattle barns
I'd hear a kind of gentle talk.

I'd move the heavy iron chain
And pull away the wooden pin;
I'd push the door a little bit
And tiptoe very softly in.

The pigeons and the yellow hens
And all the cows would stand away;
Their eyes would open wide to see
A lady in the manger hay,

If this were very long ago
And Bethlehem were here today.

And Mother held my hand and smiled—
I mean the lady would—and she
Would take the woolly blankets off
Her little boy so I could see.

His shut-up eyes would be asleep,
And he would look like our John,
And he would be all crumpled too,
And have a pinkish color on.

I'd watch his breath go in and out.
His little clothes would all be white.
I'd slip my finger in his hand
To feel how he could hold it tight.

And she would smile and say, "Take care,"
The mother, Mary, would, "Take care";
And I would kiss his little hand
And touch his hair.

While Mary put the blankets back
The gentle talk would soon begin.
And when I'd tiptoe softly out
I'd meet the wise men going in.

STRANGE TREE

Away beyond the Jarboe house
I saw a different kind of tree.
Its trunk was old and large and bent,
And I could feel it look at me.

The road was going on and on
Beyond to reach some other place.
I saw a tree that looked at me,
And yet it did not have a face.

It looked at me with all its limbs;
It looked at me with all its bark.
The yellow wrinkles on its sides
Were bent and dark.

And then I ran to get away,
But when I stopped to turn and see,

The tree was bending to the side
And leaning out to look at me.

PEOPLE GOING BY

Before they come I hear their talk
And hear their feet go on the walk.

Some go fast and some go slow,
And some of them I almost know.

In mornings they are going down
To see somebody in the town.

Or Mrs. Warner hurries past;
She has to go and come back fast.

She walks by quick and will not stop,
To go to the church with the cross on top.

I think she goes there every day
To take her rosary and pray.

And one of them is Mr. Jim—
And the big white dog that follows him.

And one is lame; that's Uncle Mells;
He takes off warts by mumbling words,
And he can lay on spells.

Or maybe night is almost come,
And Miss Jane Anne is going home.

And by her side walks Mr. Paul;
They go along with far-off looks
And hardly ever talk at all.

Or Murry's child comes up this way
To carry milk to poor Miss May

That lives in Wells's other house,
Or Joe is driving home his cows.

And some go fast and some go slow,
And some of them I almost know.

I can feel them almost speak to me,
When they pass by our tree.

BABES IN THE WOODS

The two little children that died long ago
Away in the woods on the top of a hill—
And a good little robin that knew all about it
Came with strawberry leaves in her bill,

To cover them up, and she kept very quiet
And brought the leaves one at a time, I think.
And some of the leaves would have little holes in them,
And some would be red and pink.

And these little Babes-in-the-Woods that were dead
Must have lain very still, and they heard all the talk
That the bees would be saying to more little bees,
And maybe they even could hear the ants walk.

And they could look out through a crack in the leaves
And see little bushes and some of the sky.
They could see robin coming with leaves in her mouth,
And they watched for her when she went by.

THE PICNIC

They had a picnic in the woods,
And Mother couldn't go that day,
But the twins and Brother and I could go;
We rode on the wagon full of hay.

There were more little girls than ten, I guess.
And the boy that is Joe B. Kirk was there.
He found a toad and a katydid,
And a little girl came whose name was Clare.

Miss Kate-Marie made us play a song
Called "Fare-you-well, says Johnny O'Brown."
You dance in a ring and sing it through,
And then some one kneels down.

She kissed us all and Joe B. Kirk;
But Joe B. didn't mind a bit.
He walked around and swung his arms
And seemed to be very glad of it.

Then Mr. Jim said he would play,
But Miss Marie, she told him then,
It's a game for her and the little folks,
And he could go and fish with the men.

Mr. Wells was there and he had a rope
To tie to a limb and make it swing.
And Mrs. Wells, Mr. Wells's wife,
Gave me a peach and a chicken wing.

And I had a little cherry pie
And a piece of bread, and after we'd played
Two other songs, I had some cake
And another wing and some lemonade.

THE CIRCUS

Friday came and the circus was there,
And Mother said that the twins and I
And Charles and Clarence and all of us
Could go out and see the parade go by.

And there were wagons with pictures on,
And you never could guess what they had inside,
Nobody could guess, for the doors were shut,
And there was a dog that a monkey could ride.

A man on the top of a sort of cart
Was clapping his hands and making a talk.
And the elephant came—he can step pretty far—
It made us laugh to see him walk.

Three beautiful ladies came riding by,
And each one had on a golden dress,
And each one had a golden whip.
They were queens of Sheba, I guess.

A big wild man was in a cage,
And he had some snakes going over his feet
And somebody said "He eats them alive!"
But I didn't see him eat.

MUMPS

I had a feeling in my neck,
And on the sides were two big bumps;
I couldn't swallow anything
At all because I had the mumps.

And Mother tied it with a piece,
And then she tied up Will and John,
And no one else but Dick was left
That didn't have a mump rag on.

He teased at us and laughed at us,
And said, whenever he went by,
"It's vinegar and lemon drops
And pickles!" just to make us cry.

But Tuesday Dick was very sad
And cried because his neck was sore,
And not a one said sour things
To anybody any more.

THE BRANCH

We stopped at the branch on the way to the hill.
We stopped at the water a while and played.
We hid our things by the osage tree
And took off our shoes and stockings to wade.

There is sand at the bottom that bites at your feet,
And there is a rock where the waterfall goes.
You can poke your foot in the foamy part
And feel how the water runs over your toes.

The little black spiders that walk on the top
Of the water are hard and stiff and cool.
And I saw some wiggletails going around,
And some slippery minnows that live in the pool.

And where it is smooth there is moss on a stone,
And where it is shallow and almost dry
The rocks are broken and hot in the sun,
And a rough little water goes hurrying by.

THE WORM

Dickie found a broken spade
And said he'd dig himself a well;
And then Charles took a piece of tin,
And I was digging with a shell.

Then Will said he would dig one too.
We shaped them out and made them wide,
And I dug up a piece of clod
That had a little worm inside.

We watched him pucker up himself
And stretch himself to walk away.
He tried to go inside the dirt,
But Dickie made him wait and stay.

His shining skin was soft and wet.
I poked him once to see him squirm.
And then Will said, "I wonder if
He knows that he's a worm."

And then we sat back on our feet
And wondered for a little bit.
And we forgot to dig our wells
A while, and tried to answer it.

And while we tried to find it out,
He puckered in a little wad,
And then he stretched himself again
And went back home inside the clod.

A CHILD ASLEEP

I looked for him everywhere
Because I wanted him to play;
And then I found him on his bed
Asleep, but it was day.

His eyes were shut behind the lids—
He couldn't lift them up to see.
And I looked at him very long,
And something in him looked at me.

And he was something like a cat
That is asleep, or like a dog;
Or like a thing that's in the woods
All day behind a log.

And then I was afraid of it,
Of something that was sleeping there.
I didn't even say his name,
But I came down the stair.

LITTLE BUSH

A Song

A little bush
At the picnic place,
A little bush could talk to me.

I ran away
And hid myself,
And I found a bush that could talk to me,
A smooth little bush said a word to me.

UNCLE MELLS AND THE WITCHES' TREE

He said he was tired and sore all day,
His bones were stiff and his joints were tight.
The witches had turned him into a horse,
And they rode him all that night.

They rode him out by Briartown,
And they stopped by a tree and peeled some switches;
They broke them long and peeled them keen—
Two for each of the witches.

He made the sparks fly out of the stones,
And he swam a creek where there was n't a ford,
Two witches holding onto his back,
And the moon went down in blood. . . .

When we asked him where they let him go,
And what kind of switches they were, said he,
"I would n't dare name that tree," he said,
"I would n't dare name that tree."

AT THE WATER

I liked to go to the branch today;
I liked to play with the wiggletails there.
And five little smells and one big smell
Were going round in the air.

One was the water, a little cold smell,
And one was the mud and that was more,
And one was the smell of cool wet moss,
And one was some fennel up on the shore.

And the one big smell came out of the mint,
And one was something I couldn't tell.
And the five little ones and the big one
All went together very well.

WATER NOISES

When I am playing by myself,
And all the boys are lost around,
Then I can hear the water go;
It makes a little talking sound.

Along the rocks below the tree,
I see it ripple up and wink;
And I can hear it saying on,
"And do you think? And do you think?"

A bug shoots by that snaps and ticks,
And a bird flies up beside the tree
To go into the sky to sing.
I hear it say, "Killdee, killdee!"

Or else a yellow cow comes down
To splash a while and have a drink.
But when she goes I still can hear
The water say, "And do you think?"

AMONG THE RUSHES

I saw a curly leaf and it was caught against the grassy side,
And it was tangled in the watery grasses where the branch
    is wide;
I had it for my little ark of rushes that must wait and hide.

I had it for my little Moses hidden where no one could see,
The little baby Moses that nobody knew about but me.

And I was hiding in the flags and I was waiting all the day,
And watching on the bank to see if Pharaoh's daughter
    came that way.

NUMBERS

When I can count the numbers far,
And know all the figures that there are,

Then I'll know everything, and I
Can know about the ground and sky,

And all the little bugs I see,
And I'll count the leaves on the silver-leaf tree,
And all the days that ever can be.

I'll know all the cows and sheep that pass,
And I'll know all the grass,

And all the places far away,
And I'll know everything some day.

THE DARK

There are six little houses up on the hill.

And when it is night,
There are six little windows with light.

The katydids sing and some frogs are about,
And after a while one light goes out,

And then there are five lights still.

The little frogs chirp and I hear a dog bark
Somewhere away in the dark—

Off in the dark far away somewhere
And only four houses are left up there.

And then there are three, and two, and one,
And the one little house with the light goes on

And on, and the dew gets cool,
And just for a moment there comes an owl . . .

Somebody sings three words, just three,
And five cool shivers go over the tree,
And a shiver goes over me.

A night fly comes with powdery wings
That beat on my face—it's a moth that brings

A feel of dust, and then a bright
Quick moment comes to the one little light.

But it flickers out and then it is still,
And nothing is left on the hill.

NUMBER SONG

Sixteen pigeons flew over the spire
Of the church, and as they went higher and higher

They gathered in to be twelve, and ten,
And then they were seven, and then,

When I saw them last they were four—
Wings going and then nothing more.

THE SUN AND A BIRCH TREE

As I came home through Howard's lane,
The trees were bending down with rain.

A still mist went across their tops,
And my coat was powdered gray with drops.

Then I looked in the woods to see
The limbs of the white birch tree.

It made a bright spot in the air,
And I thought the sun was shining there.

IN THE NIGHT

The light was burning very dim,
The little blaze was brown and red,
And I waked just in time to see
A panther going under the bed.

I saw him crowd his body down
To make it fit the little space.
I saw the streaks along his back,
And the bloody bubbles on his face.

Long marks of light came out of my eyes
And went into the lamp—and there
Was Something waiting in the room—
I saw it sitting on a chair.

Its only eye was shining red,
Its face was very long and gray,
Its two bent teeth were sticking out,
And all its jaw was torn away.

Its legs were flat against the chair,
Its arms were hanging like a swing.
It made its eye look into me,
But did not move or say a thing.

I tried to call and tried to scream,
But all my throat was shut and dry.
My little heart was jumping fast,
I couldn't talk or cry.

And when I'd look outside the bed
I'd see the panther going in.
The streaks were moving on his back,
The bubbles on his chin.

I couldn't help it if they came,
I couldn't save myself at all,
And so I only waited there
And turned my face against the wall.

THE GRANDMOTHER

When Grandmother comes to our house,
She sits in the chair and sews away.
She cuts some pieces just alike
And makes a quilt all day.

I watch her bite the little thread,
Or stick the needle in and out,
And then she remembers her grandmother's house,
And what her grandmother told about,

And how a very long ago—
She tells it while she cuts and strips—
We used to live in Mary-land,
And there was a water with ships.

But that was long before her day,
She says, and so I like to stand
Beside her chair, and then I ask,
"Please tell about in Mary-land."

IN MARYLAND

When it was Grandmother Annie's day,
We lived on a hill, and down below,
Beyond the pasture and the trees,
A river used to go.

The water was very wide and blue
And deep, and my! it was a sight
To see the ships go up and down,
And all the sails were white.

And Grandmother Annie used to wait
Beside the window or the door.
She never was too tired of it
To watch the river any more.

And we could hardly see across,
And the water was blue, as blue as the sky,

And all day long and all day long
We watched the little ships go by.

THE SUNDAY BONNET

It happened at Grandmother Polly's house,
And there was a bonnet put away
For Polly to wear when she went to church.
She would not wear it every day.

It had some little flowers on,
And it was standing on its head
In a bonnet box where it was safe,
Away up stairs on the company's bed.

And Grandmother Polly was going to church,
And she sent her Alice up the stair—
Alice was black—she was Evaline's child—
She waited on Polly and combed her hair.

And Alice said, "Oh, lawsie me!"
And then she cried and came running down.
And everyone went to see, and the cat
Had five little cats in the bonnet crown.

THE PEOPLE

The ants are walking under the ground,
And the pigeons are flying over the steeple,
And in between are the people.

AUTUMN FIELDS

He said his legs were stiff and sore
For he had gone some twenty-eight miles,
And he'd walked through by water gaps
And fences and gates and stiles.

He said he'd been by Logan's woods,
And up by Walton's branch and Simms,
And there were sticktights on his clothes
And little dusts of seeds and stems.

And then he sat down on the steps,
And he said the miles were on his feet.
For some of that land was tangled brush,
And some was plowed for wheat.

The rabbits were thick where he had been,
And he said he'd found some ripe papaws.
He'd rested under a white oak tree,
And for his dinner he ate red haws.

Then I sat by him on the step
To see the things that he had seen.
And I could smell the shocks and clods,
And the land where he had been.

COLD FEAR

As I came home through Drury's woods,
My face stung in the hard sleet.
The rough ground kept its frozen tracks;
They stumbled my feet.

The trees shook off the blowing frost.
The wind found out my coat was thin.
It tried to tear my clothes away.
And the cold came in.

The ice drops rattled where there was ice.
Each tree pushed back the other ones.
I did not pass a single bird,
Or anything that crawls or runs.

I saw a moth wing that was dry
And thin; it hung against a burr.
A few black leaves turned in a bush;
The grass was like cold, dead fur.

As I climbed over Howard's fence,
The wind came there with a sudden rush.
My teeth made a chattering sound,
And a bush said, "Hush!"

When I was in our house again,
With people there and fire and light,
A thought kept coming back to say,
"It will be cold out there tonight."

The clods are cold and the stones are cold,
The stiff trees shake and the hard air, . . .
And something said again to me,
"It will be cold out there."

And even when I talked myself,
And all the talk made a happy sound,
I kept remembering the wind
And the cold ground.

A LITTLE WIND

A Song

When I lay down
In a clover place,
With eyelids closed,
In a clover place,
A little wind came to my face.

One gentle wind
Blew on my mouth,
And I said, "It will quiver by.
What little wind now can it be?"
And I lay still
Where the clovers were.

But when I raised my lids to see,
Then it was a butterfly.

MR. PENNYBAKER AT CHURCH

He holds his songbook very low,
And then he stretches down his face,
And Mother said, "You mustn't watch,
He's only singing bass."

He makes his voice go walking down,
Or else he hurries twice as fast
As all the rest, but even then
He finishes the song the last.

And when I see him singing there,
I wonder if he knows it all
About Leviticus and Shem
And Deuteronomy and Saul.

THE WOLVES

When Grandmother Polly had married and gone,
But before her father had given her Clem,
Or Joe, or Sandy, or Evaline—
Before he had given her any of *them,*

She used to live in a far-away place,
In a little cabin that was her home,
And all around were bushes and trees,
And the wolves could come.

At night they ran down out of the rocks
And bristled up their trembly fur.
They came and howled by Polly's door
And showed their little white teeth at her.

A BEAUTIFUL LADY

We like to listen to her dress,
It makes a whisper by her feet.
Her little pointed shoes are gray;
She hardly lets them touch the street.

Sometimes she has a crumpled fan.
Her hat is silvered on the crown.
And there are roses by the brim
That nod and tremble up and down.

She comes along the pavement walk,
And in a moment she is gone.
She hardly ever looks at us,
But once she smiled and looked at John.

And so we run to see her pass
And watch her through the fence, and I
Can hear the others whispering,
"Miss Josephine is going by."

SHELLS IN ROCK

I've been along the quarry road,
And I have watched men digging wells,
And everywhere it was the same—
The stones were full of little shells.

And they are packed away in rock;
They're under sand and under clay;
And some one said that they were left
When the ocean went away.

I saw them in the stones that make
A church, and in a bridge.
They're hidden in the solid rock
But they show along the edge.

You see them in foundation stones;
They show in creeks and waterfalls;
And once I saw them on the jail—
More little shells in walls.

We walk on them when we walk on roads;
And they're packed under all the hills.
Suppose the sea should come back here
And gather up its shells.

HORSE

His bridle hung around the post;
The sun and the leaves made spots come down;
I looked close at him through the fence;
The post was drab and he was brown.

His nose was long and hard and still,
And on his lip were specks like chalk.
But once he opened up his eyes,
And he began to talk.

He didn't talk out with his mouth;
He didn't talk with words or noise.
The talk was there along his nose;
It seemed and then it was.

He said the day was hot and slow,
And he said he didn't like the flies;
They made him have to shake his skin,
And they got drowned in his eyes.

He said that drab was just about
The same as brown, but he was not
A post, he said, to hold a fence.
"I'm horse," he said, "that's what!"

And then he shut his eyes again.
As still as they had been before.
He said for me to run along
And not to bother him any more.

FIREFLY SONG

Firefly in the pool of water,
Bring me up a little silver,
Bring me up a star for the delight of it,
Bring me up a broken moon.

Firefly, firefly, in the water,
Bring me up a golden river,
Bring me up a fish with a light on it,
Bring me up a crooked moon.

AUGUST NIGHT

We had to wait for the heat to pass,
And I was lying on the grass,

While Mother sat outside the door,
And I saw how many stars there were.

Beyond the tree, beyond the air,
And more and more were always there.

So many that I think they must
Be sprinkled on the sky like dust.

A dust is coming through the sky!
And I felt myself begin to cry.

So many of them and so small,
Suppose I cannot know them all.

THREE DOMINICAN NUNS

One day they came; I heard their feet.
They made a tapping on the street.

And as they passed before our trees,
Their shawls blew out in curves like 3's,
And bent again in 2's and L's;

The wind blew on their rosaries
And made them ring like little bells.

MY HEART

My heart is beating up and down,
Is walking like some heavy feet.
My heart is going every day,
And I can hear it jump and beat.

At night before I go to sleep,
I feel it beating in my head;
I hear it jumping in my neck
And in the pillow on my bed.

And then I make some little words
To go along and say with it—
The men are sailing home from Troy,
And all the lamps are lit.

The men are sailing home from Troy,
And all the lamps are lit.

THE HENS

The night was coming very fast;
It reached the gate as I ran past.

The pigeons had gone to the tower of the church
And all the hens were on their perch,

Up in the barn, and I thought I heard
A piece of a little purring word.

I stopped inside, waiting and staying,
To try to hear what the hens were saying.

They were asking something, that was plain,
Asking it over and over again.

One of them moved and turned around,
Her feathers made a ruffled sound,

A ruffled sound, like a bushful of birds,
And she said her little asking words.

She pushed her head close into her wing,
But nothing answered anything.

AFTERWORD

"A butterbean is a small poem, one of a series, about a child's perceptions, remembered and seen and organized through the mind of an adult—Elizabeth as she was then." So Janet Lewis recently recalled, writing of the days when she was a young poet and Elizabeth Madox Roberts was sharing her "butterbeans" with her friends.

For well over sixty years now, "The Butterbean Tent," "On the Hill," "Christmas Morning," "The Hens," and several other butterbeans have been part of the national literary experience—staples in every well-edited anthology of literature about or for children (she emphasized that they were for "children, eighteen to eighty"). The best anthology in print, *The Golden Journey*, includes six, ranking Roberts with Blake, de la Mare, Frost, Herrick, Christina Rossetti, Stevenson, Tennyson, and Yeats. And the poems remain, as Janet Lewis observes, "as enchanting and fresh as ever."

Unfortunately, anthology encounters with only a few butterbeans have kept many readers from recognizing that the fifty-nine carefully selected and arranged poems of *Under the Tree* form a complete and beautifully realized child's-eye world of a family and a small farm town of almost a century ago. Roberts's poems are unique of their kind in seeing through the mind, eyes, and voice of a child—Walter de la Mare does it in only a handful of poems, Robert Louis Stevenson even less often. And as a poetic realization of Elizabeth Roberts's childhood Springfield, *Under the Tree* is a classic of child literature: its place is beside *The Adventures of Tom Sawyer, A Child's Garden of Verses, A Christmas Carol, Little Women, Alice in Wonderland,* and *The Wind in the Willows.*

Maurice Lesemann, an early reviewer, identified Roberts's genius as the ability to keep her memory of "the child's self that was," as almost no one can, and to speak in the child's voice without succumbing to monotony. "A child's attention is a light vagrant thing," he observes, so the writer "must labor against the tendency to become over-tight and intense in his feelings. Forms must be simple but varied; the rhymes must be inevitable; they must fall in the casual inevitability of speech." This leaves the less obvious difficulty: "The impossible—the almost unattainable thing is that sudden arrest of the child's mood, the child's way of seeing, which grown-ups have forgotten and may catch and hold again only for a moment now and then as if by some sort of intelligent magic."

This achievement required in Roberts's words, "the little girl, myself, the 'I' of the verses"—the sensitive and searching voice we meet again in Ellen Chesser, the adolescent daughter of tenant farmers in the fictional classic, *The Time of Man*.

The little girl and the poetic genius give us, in poetry, Elizabeth Roberts's childhood in Springfield—"a little old drowsy town" in a "rolling country," she advised her illustrator—a world with a past, a landscape, a varied citizenry, institutions, customs, rituals, games, illnesses, stories, fantasies, and moods ranging from fear to wonder and joy. "It is the only autobiography I shall ever write," she said.

As poems their achievement is substantial. William Jay Smith, himself an accomplished writer of children's verse, observed in 1981: "The poems in *Under the Tree* are balanced on the knife edge between innocence and maturity, life and death, dream and waking, sanity and madness. For all their civility (and the heroine of this poetry is every bit as civil as Alice), there is terror below the calm surface: the panther in the shadows of the bedroom, the strange tree looking back ('And yet it did not have a face'). There is a constant double vision of earth and air, of world and universe, of microcosm and macrocosm. And throughout there is magnificent mastery."

Who is Elizabeth Madox Roberts? She was born in 1881 in Perryville, Kentucky, but her family soon settled in nearby Springfield, the county seat of Washington County, where Lincoln's parents were married—a few miles in one direction from the site of the pioneer Fort Harrod, in the other from the Old Kentucky Home of Stephen Foster's song. Her forebears were pioneers. Her father fought with the Confederacy, then became a teacher, lawyer, engineer, and surveyor. Her mother taught school. Her five brothers and her sister figure prominently in *Under the Tree.*

Elizabeth's childhood wish to be a poet was frustrated for years by frail health and lack of money for an education; she did not get to college until she was thirty-five. For some years she had taught in one- and two-room schools and in the fourth-grade classroom of Springfield's graded school. At the University of Chicago she began writing prose accounts of her childhood. Before long the first poem appeared, then others, pulled from her muff and passed to Poetry Club friends. Years later the club's adviser, Robert Morss Lovett, wrote: "I can hear today the light, sweet voice of Elizabeth Roberts reading her children's poems with the perfect touch of childhood shaded with humor."

In 1921, Miss Roberts returned to Kentucky to write—over the next twenty years seven novels, including *The Great Meadow* about the settling of Kentucky, two volumes of stories, and another book of poems. Sherwood Anderson, Allen Tate, Robert Penn Warren, Ford Madox Ford, and Jesse Stuart were unreserved in praise of her work. By the 1930s she had become a leading figure in American literature.

Miss Roberts never married but, back in Springfield, often played with the children of the neighborhood—escorting them to the fair or joining them in teasing jacksnipes out of their holes and observing "another tragedy of bug-dom." When her niece Georgine visited, she rejoiced in fantasies that reminded her of the "pretend" people she and her brothers and sister had created in the 1880s.

Under the Tree was first published in 1922; illustrations and a few more poems were added in the 1930 edition and appeared in subsequent editions. A few discarded butterbeans appear in *I Touched White Clover,* a special 1981 issue of *Kentucky Poetry Review.* Other child poems are included in *Song in the Meadow* (1940).

WILLIAM H. SLAVICK